WORLD WINDOWS

School Rules

HEINLE
CENGAGE Learning™

YSG Young & Son Global, Inc.
A YBM COMPANY

What are the rules at your school?

Contents

Vocabulary 4

Rules at School 6

In Class 7

In the Cafeteria 9

In the Hallway 10

In the Library 11

Follow the Rules 12

Summary 14

Song 15

Index 16

Vocabulary

rules

raise

listen

line up
walk
quiet

There are rules at school.

Raise your hand in class.

Listen to the teacher in class.

Line up in the cafeteria.

Do not run in the hallway.
Walk in the hallway.

Do not shout in the library.
Be quiet in the library.

Follow the school rules!

They keep you safe and help you learn.

Summary

What are these school rules?

Song

The School Rules

When you're at school, when you're at school,
Follow these rules! Follow these rules!
Listen to the teacher! Listen to the teacher!
Raise your hand! Raise your hand!

When you're at school, when you're at school,
Follow these rules! Follow these rules!
Walk in the hallway! Walk in the hallway!
Please line up! Please line up!

Index

follow, 12

line up, 9

listen, 8

quiet, 11

raise, 7

rules, 6, 12

run, 10

school, 6, 12

shout, 11

walk, 10